CHALLENGES FOR LGBTQ TEENS

By Martha Lundin

ReferencePoint
Press®

San Diego, CA

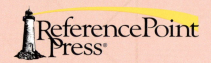

For more information, contact:
ReferencePoint Press, Inc.
PO Box 27779
San Diego, CA 92198
www.ReferencePointPress.com

Content Consultant: Ericka Burns, Founder of Sacramento Peers on Prevention

LIBRARY OF CONGRESS CATALOGING-IN-PUBLICATION DATA

Names: Lundin, Martha, 1993- author.
Title: Challenges for LGBTQ teens / Martha Lundin.
Description: San Diego : ReferencePoint Press, 2021. | Series: Teen problems | Includes
    bibliographical references and index. | Audience: Grades 10-12
Identifiers: LCCN 2020003699 (print) | LCCN 2020003700 (eBook) | ISBN 9781682829639
    (hardcover) | ISBN 9781682829646 (eBook)
Subjects: LCSH: Lesbian teenagers--United States--Juvenile literature. | Gay teenagers--
    United States--Juvenile literature. | Bisexual teenagers--United States--Juvenile literature.
    | Transgender youth--United States--Juvenile literature. | Bullying--Prevention--Juvenile
    literature.
Classification: LCC HQ76.26 .L86 2020 (print) | LCC HQ76.26 (eBook) | DDC 306.760973--
    dc23
LC record available at https://lccn.loc.gov/2020003699
LC eBook record available at https://lccn.loc.gov/2020003700

CONTENTS

CHALLENGES FOR LGBTQ+ TEENS

Jess is bisexual. She is a sophomore in high school. Jess recently came out to her close friends, who were all supportive. But Jess doesn't know how to tell her parents about her sexuality. She doesn't think they will kick her out, but her family belongs to a large religious community. Jess is worried that her parents will not accept her. For now, Jess has decided not to tell her parents about her sexuality. Coming out at school was hard enough.

Jess's friends are great. She joined a gender-sexuality alliance (GSA) at her high school. In this group, she can hang out with other students who are gay, lesbian, or questioning. Jess likes having a community because her school often feels unsafe. Since she came out as bisexual, some of Jess's peers started spreading rumors. They said Jess slept with a lot

Gender-sexuality alliances or gay-straight alliances (GSAs) exist in many schools. These groups allow members of the LGBTQ+ community and their allies to come together in a supportive environment.

of people. Her peers said all bisexual people are cheaters. Girls in Jess's class told her not to hit on them. Jess did not know how to tell her peers that they were wrong about her. She was self-conscious. Jess did not want to go to the administrators because she heard from other students that they were not helpful. Jess was beginning to feel depressed. She did not want to be harassed at school. She worked with a trusted teacher to make a plan to talk to the school counselor.

TERMINOLOGY

Lesbian, gay, bisexual, transgender, and questioning or queer (LGBTQ+) teens face a wide variety of challenges in the United States. Learning about these challenges may include terminology that is new to some people. Understanding these terms is one way to help LGBTQ+ teens.

Gender identity describes the deeply felt understanding a person has about their gender. Sex is based on biological and physical genital appearance. The two most common sex assignments are male and female. People can also be intersex. Many people are cisgender, which means they identify with the sex they were assigned at birth. For example, a cisgender girl was assigned female at birth. Other people are transgender. They do not identify with the sex they were assigned. A transgender girl was assigned male at birth; however, she does not identify as a boy, she identifies as a girl.

Sexual orientation describes who a person is attracted to romantically or sexually. A lesbian is a woman who is attracted to other women. A gay man is attracted to other men. However, women can also identify as gay, since the term simply means that a person is attracted to people of the same sex. Bisexual people are attracted to the same and other genders. Pansexual people are attracted to people of all genders. Asexual people do not feel sexual attraction to any person.

Sexual orientation and gender identity are two different things. Sexual orientation is who a person is attracted to. Gender identity describes a person's gender.

Gender identity and sexual orientation are separate. Many people have a sexual orientation and gender identity. Agender people experience no gender identity. Scientist Chanda Prescod-Weinstein is a "pansexual agender cissex woman." Prescod-Weinstein says, "I do a lot of advocacy for marginalized people in the sciences and have been an active member of the National Society of Black Physicists for nearly fifteen years."[1]

Some people know their sexual orientation and gender identity early in their life. But others find their identity later on. That was the experience of Britta Gregor Krabill, a librarian who identifies as sexually fluid. In an interview, she said, "It's important for people questioning their sexuality to see that it's not abnormal for sexual orientation to evolve as we get older. Finding your orientation changing doesn't mean that there's anything wrong with you."[2]

> "It's important for people questioning their sexuality to see that it's not abnormal for sexual orientation to evolve as we get older. Finding your orientation changing doesn't mean that there's anything wrong with you."[2]
>
> —*Britta Gregor Krabill, a librarian who identifies as sexually fluid*

Many young people use the word *queer* to describe their gender and sexual orientation. It is used as an umbrella term, or a term that covers a wide range of identities. But the word used to have a negative meaning. It was once used to attack people with these identities. Because of this, some older LGBTQ+ people do not use the term to describe themselves. In this book, the word *queer* may appear as an umbrella term for all LGBTQ+ people. But its use does not discount the experiences of LGBTQ+ people for whom the word has been a source of pain.

Some people believe that people can only be male or female. This two-gender system is called the binary. However, both gender and sexuality are much more complicated than male or female, gay or straight. People can be intersex, transgender, genderqueer, gender-fluid, or agender. They can be straight, bisexual, pansexual, or asexual. Intersex individuals are sometimes born with ambiguous genitalia. Other times they have chromosomal differences besides the typically female XX or the typically male XY. Genderqueer and gender-fluid people are nonbinary. They do not identify with either male or female.

Psychologists say it is possible to discover new aspects of sexual attraction and gender identity. However, they also stress that it is not possible to force a person to be straight or cisgender. Gender identity and sexual orientation can change over time. These changes can occur because of several reasons. One is increased knowledge. People cannot name a feeling without knowing the language to describe it. As people continue to explore their identity, the words they use to describe themselves may change. Payton Quinn is a trans, gender-fluid, nonbinary person. In an interview, they echoed this feeling of constant change, saying, "My gender is an evolving thing, like my sexuality, the more I explore it the more it changes. The only reason why I feel I should put a label on it is just to make

> "My gender is an evolving thing, like my sexuality, the more I explore it the more it changes. The only reason why I feel I should put a label on it is just to make it easier for other people."[3]
>
> —Payton Quinn, a trans, gender-fluid, nonbinary person

Marriage equality in the United States, which became law in 2015, was an important step for LGBTQ+ rights. However, the LGBTQ+ community still faces challenges to equality.

it easier for other people."[3] Additionally, labels a person once identified with may not fit anymore. On the other hand, many people feel that their sexual orientation and gender identity do not change.

Because they change depending on gender, pronouns are an important way for LGBTQ+ teens to establish their identity.

A cisgender girl might use the pronouns *she*, *her*, and *hers*. A transgender man might use the pronouns *he*, *him*, and *his*. Some pronouns are gender neutral. One such pronoun is *they*. In 2019, the Merriam-Webster dictionary named *they* the word of the year. This recognized the increased prominence of gender identity in today's society.

Challenges for LGBTQ+ teens have changed over time. There have been many advancements in LGBTQ+ rights in the twenty-first century. However, teens continue to face challenges at home, at school, and in their communities. LGBTQ+ advocates are working to help all LGBTQ+ teens feel safe and confident with their identities. These advocates come from around the country and are of all ages. For example, Sameer Jha is a fifteen-year-old queer, gender nonconforming activist. In a 2017 interview, they said their ethnicity informs their work as an activist: "As a queer person of color who traces my heritage to a country in which homosexuality is punishable by death, I want to use my privilege as an American citizen with a supportive family to raise awareness and fight for the people who can't."[4]

CHAPTER ONE

WHAT ARE THE CHALLENGES?

LGBTQ+ teens face various challenges. Many of these challenges show up most noticeably in school. Fewer than half of US states have legal protections for LGBTQ+ students against bullying and discrimination. The challenges LGBTQ+ teens face in school have a direct impact on their mental and physical health.

DISCRIMINATION

The Williams Institute is part of the University of California, Los Angeles's Law School. It specializes in LGBTQ+ studies. According to the Williams Institute, there are 3.2 million LGBTQ+ youth ages eight to eighteen living in the United States. Many of these youth attend public schools. However, each state has different antidiscrimination laws. Some have explicit protections for LGBTQ+ students, but many do not.

Only twenty states and Washington, DC, have protections regarding sexual orientation and/or gender identity. Some states

Many schools do not have legal protections for LGBTQ+ students. This can lead to bullying.

only list sexual orientation. Others include gender and sexual orientation under the broader umbrella term *sex*. Jocelyn Samuels is the executive director of the Williams Institute. She believes all LGBTQ+ students should be protected from sex discrimination. Samuels explains, "Sexual orientation and gender identity discrimination are forms of sex stereotyping because they are based on stereotypical notions of who your romantic partner should be, how you should appear, what kinds of mannerisms you should have."[5] Not all legislators agree with her.

States and school districts must make their own definition of what sex discrimination includes. That means most states do not have protections for LGBTQ+ youth. The Williams Institute estimates 55 percent of LGBTQ+ youth attend schools without protections against discrimination for gender identity and sexual orientation. Lack of protection means students can legally be discriminated against for their sexual orientation or gender identity. School policies sometimes exclude LGBTQ+ students.

For example, some policies target transgender students. Many are not allowed to use the bathrooms or locker rooms that match their gender identity. Instead, they are forced to use the bathroom that matches their assigned sex, or they must use a single-stall bathroom in the nurse's office. For transgender students, their assigned sex feels wrong. When they are forced to use a different restroom or locker room than their peers, they feel singled out. Some feel these policies open up other forms of harassment and violence by peers.

Transgender students face particular challenges around bathrooms and locker rooms. Some schools may force students to use the bathroom for their assigned sex rather than their gender identity.

Transgender students are not the only students harmed by school policies. Many LGBTQ+ students are prevented from forming student organizations. Even those students who are allowed to form gay-straight alliances or gender-sexuality alliances (GSAs) still face discrimination in other school-sponsored events. A GSA is a student organization that brings together LGBTQ+ students and their allies. Allies are non-LGBTQ+ students who want to work to support their LGBTQ+ peers and friends. Even in schools where GSAs are present, there can be school policies that discriminate against students.

GLSEN, formerly known as the Gay, Lesbian & Straight Education Network, is an organization for students and school staff and administrators. It works to create a safer environment for LGBTQ+ students. Every two years, GLSEN conducts a national school climate study. In the study, it asks students about bullying and harassment as well as what kind of school policies exist. GLSEN uses the information in the survey to provide recommendations to school administrators and state and national legislators. In the 2017 School Climate Survey, 12 percent of respondents said they were not allowed to attend a dance with a partner of the same gender. Additionally, 13 percent of LGBTQ+ students said they were not allowed to wear clothing that supported LGBTQ+ issues. Some students were even prevented from including LGBTQ+ topics in assignments. One student who responded to the survey wrote, "When I tried to make one of my open-ended projects LGBTQ+ related, the teacher told me that it was inappropriate, and forced me to restart the project."[6]

When school policies do not protect LGBTQ+ students, other forms of harassment become more common. Additionally, it becomes less likely that LGBTQ+ students will receive help from administrators. Unsafe school environments have repercussions for LGBTQ+ youth far outside school walls.

HARASSMENT

Harassment takes many forms. It can happen in person and online. Wherever it happens, it has a negative effect on LGBTQ+ students' participation in classes and extracurricular activities.

In the 2017 School Climate Survey, 95 percent of LGBTQ+ students reported that they had heard homophobic remarks—derogatory comments about LGBTQ+ people—in school. Ninety-eight percent of them had heard the term *gay* used in a negative way. These remarks did not come only from peers. They also came from teachers and administrators. Some teachers made comments about LGBTQ+ people in general. For example, in an interview, Bianca L., a bisexual student in Alabama, said, "My biology

"DON'T SAY GAY"

Six US states prevent teachers from including LGBTQ+ material in their lessons. These laws, sometimes known as Don't Say Gay rules, are targeted at prohibiting inclusive sex-education for LGBTQ+ students. However, many are worded so that the rule can apply to other subjects as well, such as English and history classes. Some students have even been told they cannot form a gay-straight alliance or gender-sexuality alliance (GSA). Many of these rules were created under the false belief that talking about LGBTQ+ people would turn students gay or transgender. Studies show that LGBTQ+ students in states with Don't Say Gay laws are more likely to face harassment and discrimination at school.

Sometimes teachers are the perpetrators of harassment of LGBTQ+ teens. This can range from not allowing students to write about LGBTQ+ topics in class to making disparaging remarks.

teacher my freshman year would bring in kids who were wearing short shorts or weird sweaters and say, 'You'd better take that off, you're going to look gay.'[7] Another student from Rhode Island said that after she came out, her teachers treated her differently. She said, "Before I came out, I

> "My biology teacher my freshman year would bring in kids who were wearing short shorts or weird sweaters and say, 'You'd better take that off, you're going to look gay.'"[7]
>
> —*Bianca L., student*

was respected by my teachers. But soon after I came out, some of my teachers started to give me dirty looks, not calling on me in class, avoiding me at any cost and refusing to give me help after school. I actually had a teacher, as I walked by his desk, whisper under his breath 'God forgive her,' as if I were sinning just being alive."[8]

Even when schools have policies to protect students from verbal harassment, LGBTQ+ students are not always protected. One student reported, "While my school does have policies against hate speech and harassment, the administration usually takes no action against students reported for such things."[9]

Phrases such as "That's so gay" create an atmosphere of hostility for LGBTQ+ students. Verbal harassment, on the other hand, is directed at one student in particular. Approximately 70 percent of LGBTQ+ students reported direct verbal harassment. One student in the 2017 survey wrote, "A student called me a faggot at school right in front of a teacher and the teacher did nothing."[10] In addition to verbal harassment at school, LGBTQ+ students are also at risk online. Nearly 49 percent of LGBTQ+ students reported electronic harassment in the past year.

Both types of hostility make LGBTQ+ students feel unsafe. Danielle Wilcox is a board member for the Center for Equality in Sioux Falls, South Dakota. She notes, "Too many of the LGBT youth in our community are subject to slurs and jokes, or even physical attacks, that make them feel alone."[11] Approximately 59 percent of LGBTQ+ students said they felt unsafe at school. As a result, nearly 35 percent of students reported missing at least one day of school in the last month due to fear of harassment at the time of the survey. LGBTQ+ students will go to extreme lengths to avoid harassment. One student wrote: "I lived in fear every day I got on that bus. I started walking to school because after a while, I wouldn't even take the bus anymore, it was just like my stomach was in knots. I had to live every day trying to avoid being harassed."[12]

Outside of school, LGBTQ+ youth face rejection from family and faith leaders. There are still many adults in the United States who do not understand sexual orientation and gender identity. As a result, they feel their LGBTQ+-identified child is lying about their identity. Some families may even seek out a way to change their child's sexual orientation or gender identity. The practice of trying to change a person's gender identity or sexual orientation is called conversion therapy. Conversion therapy is sometimes called reparative therapy or ex-gay therapy. Conversion therapy is still in practice, even though a majority of mental health

People across the country have campaigned to end harmful conversion therapy. On March 21, 2019, high school students in Minnesota marched to the State Capitol building to show their support for a ban.

professionals have determined it neither works nor is safe. Many mental health professionals say it is harmful to call the practice therapy at all. Several states in the United States are working to make conversion therapy illegal.

VIOLENCE

LGBTQ+ students face more challenges than verbal harassment. Many face violence in unsupportive schools. In the 2017 survey, nearly 29 percent of LGBTQ+ students said they were pushed or shoved in the past year because of their sexual orientation. Transgender students often experience violence in bathrooms. As adults, black trans women continue to face increased violence. The life expectancy of a black trans woman is thirty-five. In contrast, the average life span of all women in the United Sates is eighty-one.

More than half of LGBTQ+ students reported sexual harassment in the past year in the School Climate Survey. Students said they had been groped, or touched inappropriately. In another study, one student noted, "I've been shoved into lockers, and sometimes people will just push up on me to check if I have boobs."[13] For transgender students, this is particularly uncomfortable.

LGBTQ+ teens continue to be at risk in college. They are more likely to be the victims of sexual assault and rape. According to a University of Michigan

CONVERSION THERAPY

For centuries, same-sex desire was believed to be an illness. Efforts to change a person's sexuality are not new. Conversion therapy is the practice of trying to change a person's sexual or gender identity. The purpose is to make a person heterosexual if they are gay or cisgender if they are transgender. Through the late 1900s and into the 2000s, methods have stayed largely the same. Sometimes conversion therapy is conducted by faith leaders. Darren Calhoun is a black gay man. When he was seventeen, a faith leader tried to change Darren's sexual orientation. Darren worked with the pastor for two years. In an article, Calhoun wrote, "Over time, my pastor directed me to quit school so that I could focus all my energy on his instructions." Conversion therapy practitioners use shame and even electric shocks to attempt to change a person's identity. However, the overwhelming majority of mental health advocates agree that conversion therapy does not work. Further, the practice is harmful to LGBTQ+ people, especially youth.

Darren Calhoun, "How I Survived 'Ex-Gay' Conversion Therapy," Colorlines, June 14, 2018. www.colorlines.com.

Facing hostility at school can affect physical and mental health. It can also cause LGBTQ+ teens to skip school, which negatively affects grades and schoolwork.

survey, LGBTQ+ students are twice as likely to be sexually assaulted as their non-LGBTQ+ peers. However, policies that protect LGBTQ+ students specifically are lacking.

More than half of LGBTQ+ students did not report physical harassment or assault to school administrators. One reason for this is a fear of being blamed for the harassment. A student

Many LGBTQ+ students do not report harassment to school administrators. They worry they will be blamed for the actions or that administrators won't take action.

wrote, "I've only gone to school staff once after [being groped] and I was questioned if I had done something to provoke this sort of response from my peers."[14] According to the School Climate Survey, 60 percent of students who went to administrators said school leaders did not help them.

Researchers have found that a hostile school climate makes LGBTQ+ teens more likely to face additional challenges outside of school. A hostile climate at school affects mental and physical health. Additionally, a hostile school and home life means LGBTQ+ youth are more likely to experience homelessness. Housing insecurity has negative effects on youth mental health. LGBTQ+ youth are more likely to abuse drugs and alcohol. As of 2019, researchers and LGBTQ+ activists are seeing rising rates of mental illness for LGBTQ+ youth. They say something must be done. Jessica Valenti, a columnist for the *Guardian*, wrote: "It's no longer good enough to remind LGBT kids that 'it gets better.' We need to figure out more legal, safe alternatives for those who can't wait that long."[15] The consequences of not providing support to LGBTQ+ youth can be life-threatening.

"It's no longer good enough to remind LGBT kids that 'it gets better.' We need to figure out more legal, safe alternatives for those who can't wait that long."[15]

—*Jessica Valenti,*
Guardian *columnist*

CHAPTER TWO

HOW DO THESE CHALLENGES AFFECT TEENS?

The challenges LGBTQ+ teens face have many negative effects. One of the largest effects is worsened mental health. LGBTQ+ youth face higher rates of mental illness than their heterosexual and cisgender peers. Mental illness can lead to unhealthy coping mechanisms and an increased risk of suicide.

DEPRESSION AND ANXIETY

LGBTQ+ teens face repeated stresses every day. These stresses are different than those faced by non-LGBTQ+ teens. The stresses LGBTQ+ teens face often have to do with their sexual or gender identity. Minority stress theory explains the effect these stresses have on LGBTQ+ teens as well as other minority populations. Scientists study how prejudice and violence affect people of color and LGBTQ+ populations in the United States.

Discrimination and other challenges cause high rates of mental illnesses in the LGBTQ+ community. These include depression, anxiety, suicidal ideation, and more.

They saw that these populations faced unique stressors because of their identity. Ilan Meyer works at the Williams Institute. While he was a researcher at Columbia University, he wrote, "Stigma, prejudice, and discrimination create a hostile and stressful social environment that causes mental health problems."[16]

Prejudice and stigma do not always show up as major experiences. Sometimes the acts are small. These acts are called microaggressions. For example, using the wrong pronouns for a transgender person can be harmful. In an interview, a student named Acanthus said, "It doesn't seem like a big deal [when someone uses the wrong pronouns], but eventually you bruise."[17] As a result of prejudice and social stigma, LGBTQ+ youth may begin to feel isolated from the rest of their community and family. A 2019 study found that LGBTQ+ youth face higher rates of mental illness than heterosexual and cisgender youth.

> "It doesn't seem like a big deal [when someone uses the wrong pronouns], but eventually you bruise."[17]
>
> —Acanthus R., student

Approximately 18 percent of lesbian and gay youth met the requirements for major depression, a mental disorder that involves persistent feelings of sadness and a loss of interest in previously enjoyable activities. In contrast, only 8.2 percent of heterosexual youth met the same criteria. Additionally, lesbian, gay, and bisexual youth were nearly three times as likely to be diagnosed with post-traumatic stress disorder (PTSD), a mental disorder that involves a person experiencing anxiety and flashbacks after a traumatic event.

People cope with mental illness in a variety of ways. Those individuals who have supportive families and social circles are more likely to have healthy coping mechanisms. Healthy coping

Having a support group is important for LGBTQ+ youth. Some parents wear "Free Mom Hugs" or "Free Dad Hugs" T-shirts at Pride festivals to help LGBTQ+ people whose parents aren't supportive.

mechanisms include journaling, moderate exercise, and doodling in a notebook. However, LGBTQ+ youth are less likely to have social support. Rejection from family or friends causes a drop in self-esteem. Perceived or real rejection causes LGBTQ+ youth to seek escape from the rejection. They are more likely to develop unhealthy coping mechanisms such as substance abuse and self-harm.

Unhealthy coping mechanisms may put people in danger of causing harm to themselves or others. LGBTQ+ teens have

BULLYING AND LGBTQ+ YOUTH

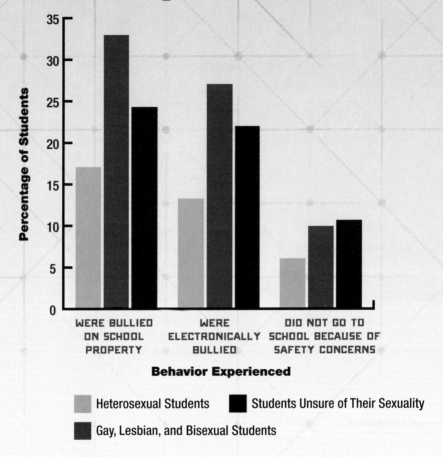

Source: Laura Kann, Tim McManus, William A. Harris et al., "Youth Risk Behavior Surveillance—United States, 2017," Centers for Disease Control and Prevention: Morbidity and Mortality Weekly Report, June 15, 2018. www.cdc.gov.

In 2017, the Centers for Disease Control and Prevention (CDC) conducted the Youth Risk Behavior Survey. The survey asked students in high schools across the United States whether they had experienced certain behaviors in the last twelve months. Students could identify themselves as heterosexual, gay or lesbian, bisexual, or not sure.

higher rates of alcohol and substance abuse. Many LGBTQ+ youth turn to drugs and alcohol after coming out. Drugs and alcohol may dull feelings of rejection or stigma. LGBTQ+ youth also show higher rates of sexually transmitted infections (STIs). LGBTQ+ youth may look for ways to validate themselves. One way they may try to validate themselves is by engaging in sex with multiple partners in a short amount of time. LGBTQ+ youth may not use safe-sex practices. This leads to higher rates of STIs. While sexual activity can be a way for LGBTQ+ youth to feel confident in their identity, unprotected sex and sex with multiple partners increases the risk of infection in both the person and their partner. LGBTQ+ youth may engage in unprotected sex as a way to forget about an unsafe home or school environment. When youth engage in unprotected sex, counselors sometimes label this behavior as self-harm.

SUICIDE RATES

LGBTQ+ youth are more likely to attempt suicide than their non-LGBTQ+ peers. Suicide risk is influenced by many factors, including social acceptance and whether parents place LGBTQ+ youth in conversion therapy. Identifying as LGBTQ+ does not itself raise the risk of suicide. Rather, it is the stresses that LGBTQ+ people encounter that raise the risk of suicide. Minority stress can increase this risk. The US Department of Health and Human Services released a statement on suicide rates of LGBTQ+ people. It stated: "Suicidal behaviors in LGBT populations appear to be related to 'minority stress', which stems from the cultural and social prejudice attached to minority sexual orientation and gender identity. This stress includes individual experiences of prejudice or discrimination, such as family rejection, harassment, bullying, violence, and victimization." The statement goes on to describe how society can have an impact on LGBTQ+ people: "Increasingly recognized as an aspect of minority stress is 'institutional discrimination' resulting from laws and public policies that create inequities or omit LGBT people from benefits and protections afforded others."[18]

According to a 2018 study, approximately 18 percent of cisgender girls and 10 percent of cisgender boys have ever tried to take their own life. The statistics for transgender youth are dramatically higher. The figure for transgender females was 30 percent, and the figure for transgender males was 51 percent. The percentage for adolescents who identified as neither male nor female was 42 percent. Additionally, suicide attempts from LGBTQ+ youth are more likely to require medical attention than attempts by non-LGBTQ+ youth.

Suicide rates go up when LGBTQ+ youth go through sexual orientation or gender identity change efforts. Youth may be pressured by family, community, and religious leaders to change their identity. Psychologists and doctors agree conversion therapy does not work. It is not possible for a gay person to

While identifying as LGBTQ+ does not increase suicide risk, the challenges that LGBTQ+ people face can increase this risk. Rejection by family, friends, or religious leaders can lead to feelings of isolation.

become heterosexual. A transgender person cannot change their identity to their assigned sex.

When youth are told their identity is wrong, they may develop self-loathing, depression, and anxiety. Some youth may sincerely want to change their identity. When conversion therapy does not work, LGBTQ+ youth may feel even worse about themselves.

Youth in conversion therapy may be forced to stay at a location far away from family and friends. This creates an added stress for them. Some youth require hospitalization because of the stress. One survivor of conversion therapy said hospitalization was what ultimately saved them: "The culmination of my year in conversion therapy was severe major depression that [led] to suicidal ideation. . . . Nearly 50 percent of youth in involuntary conversion therapy [die by] suicide. Individual circumstance is the only reason I got out."[19]

> "The culmination of my year in conversion therapy was severe major depression that [led] to suicidal ideation. . . . Nearly 50 percent of youth in involuntary conversion therapy [die by] suicide. Individual circumstance is the only reason I got out."[19]
>
> —Sage Guttschow, a conversion therapy survivor

According to a 2018 study conducted by the Family Acceptance Project, rates of suicide increase dramatically when youth are exposed to efforts to change their identity. Fifty-three percent of respondents reported experiencing conversion therapy or related efforts to change their sexual or gender identity. Dr. Caitlin Ryan, the director of the Family Acceptance Project, said parents may be trying to help their children, but the hurt that conversion therapy causes cannot be avoided.

She said in an interview, "Although parents and religious leaders who try to change a child's LGBT identity may be motivated by attempts to 'protect' their children, these rejecting behaviors instead undermine an LGBT child's sense of self-worth, contribute to self-destructive behaviors that significantly increase risk and inhibit self-care, which includes constricting their ability to make a living."[20]

Across all responses in the 2018 study, 22 percent reported trying to take their own life. However, when youth were exposed to conversion therapy, those numbers rose. Forty-eight percent of respondents said they tried to take their own life when parents attempted to change the youth's orientation. An even higher percentage of people said they tried to take their own life when parents and a religious or community leader had tried to change the LGBTQ+ youth's identity.

The study provided researchers with further evidence of the harm conversion therapy causes. After the report was published, coauthor Dr. Stephen Russell from the University of Texas at Austin wrote, "We now have even more dramatic evidence of the lasting personal and social cost of subjecting young people to so-called 'change' or 'conversion' therapies."[21]

Family rejection and exposure to conversion therapy causes LGBTQ+ youth to seek out escapes from that rejection. Some

LGBTQ+ youth may feel like the only solution is to leave home. As a result, homelessness for LGBTQ+ youth is a major issue.

LIVING WITHOUT A HOME

Researchers estimate 40 percent of homeless youth identify as LGBTQ+. Black LGBTQ+ youth face a higher risk of homelessness than white LGBTQ+ youth. LGBTQ+ youth experience housing insecurity for a variety of reasons. Some report being kicked out of their homes. Others run away from abusive families or foster homes. That's what happened with Alex, a transgender teen in Texas. Alex said in an interview, "My mother and I would argue and then I would run away. I would run away so much that Child Protective Services eventually took me away."[22]

> "My mother and I would argue and then I would run away. I would run away so much that Child Protective Services eventually took me away."[22]
>
> —*Alex, a transgender teen in the Texas foster system*

Not having a home is hard on all people. LGBTQ+ youth face increased risk of sexual abuse and substance abuse. As a result, LGBTQ+ youth face a higher risk of premature death due to overdose, murder, or suicide. Many unhoused youth turn to sex work or labor trafficking in order to eat or find temporary shelter. Labor trafficking is forced labor. According to a 2018 survey, nearly half of homeless LGBTQ+ youth were victims of labor trafficking. Some youth said their drivers' licenses were taken away so they could not leave. Eric Wright, a sociologist at the University of Georgia and leader of the survey, said, "The labor trafficking was much more prevalent than the sex trafficking."[23] Sex work and sex trafficking are different. Sex trafficking means forcing a person to have sex with people. Sex work is consensual. A person who engages in sex work has sex for money. Survival sex is not uncommon in unhoused communities. People who engage in survival sex have sex in exchange for money. The money is used to pay for necessary things such as food. Many unhoused LGBTQ+ youth feel they have no choice. One gay nineteen-year-old Latino said in a 2015 interview, "If you have no food in your stomach, if you have no transportation, . . . [y]ou put your pride to the side, you throw everything out the window and you forget who you are and you forget what you're doing and you learn to be someone else."[24]

But finding solutions to help LGBTQ+ youth find permanent, supportive homes is difficult. Alphonso David is the president of the Human Rights Campaign (HRC). HRC is an organization that works to improve LGBTQ+ rights. In a speech, David said, "On any given day, as many as 10,000 LGBTQ young people do not have a safe place to sleep. In some U.S. cities, 30 percent of the homeless adult population is LGBTQ. The faces behind these numbers reflect our community's most vulnerable—our youth, our transgender siblings, and people living with HIV."[25]

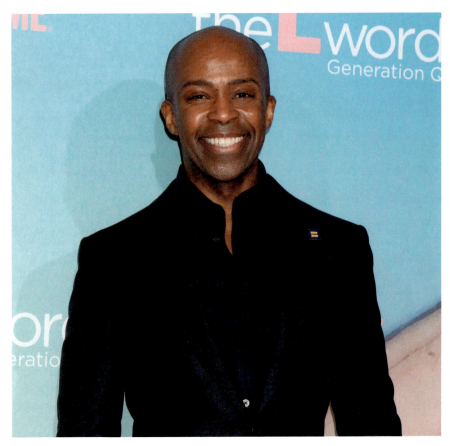

Alphonso David is a civil rights lawyer and advocate. He became president of the Human Rights Campaign (HRC) in 2019.

Unhoused LGBTQ+ youth lack stability. Their focus must often be on finding food or a place to sleep. As a result, unhoused LGBTQ+ youth are less likely to finish high school. There are added stigmas attached to individuals who do not receive their diploma. LGBTQ+ youth who face housing insecurity have fewer resources and face additional social stigma compared to youth who have a stable home environment.

Some solutions to housing insecurity include host-home programs and rapid rehousing. Host-home programs are similar to foster care. Host families volunteer to take in LGBTQ+ youth experiencing a gap in housing. Host families usually receive LGBTQ+-specific training in order to better serve the specific needs of LGBTQ+ youth. Rapid rehousing is an option for older LGBTQ+ youth. Rapid rehousing involves giving an apartment to an LGBTQ+ youth in their own name. A stipend covers the cost of rent for up to two years as the youth works to find employment. Case workers help the youth find jobs or apply to colleges. Preliminary studies show these types of programs have a high success rate in providing stable housing for LGBTQ+ youth.

THE FOSTER SYSTEM

Children enter the foster care system for various reasons, such as the death of parents, neglect, abuse, and incarceration, among other situations. For LGBTQ+ children, sometimes their parents do not want to care for them. LGBTQ+ kids may face rejection when they come out. For some, rejection turns into mistreatment. Mistreatment can include physical and emotional abuse.

LGBTQ+ children are overrepresented in the foster system. Approximately 20 percent of children in foster care in Los Angeles identified as LGBTQ+, compared to 7 to 10 percent of the general population. LGBTQ+ children in foster care may continue to face discrimination from foster parents or group homes. LGBTQ+ children are more likely to bounce between homes than their non-LGBTQ+ peers. LGBTQ+ foster children are twice as likely to report physical and verbal abuse from other foster children and guardians than non-LGBTQ+ foster youth.

CHAPTER THREE

HOW DO THESE CHALLENGES AFFECT SOCIETY?

LGBTQ+ teens face challenges that often stem from larger social systems. These systems affect more than LGBTQ+ youth. Both LGBTQ+ youth and adults face issues in the foster and adoption system and with health care providers. As of 2019, there is no federal antidiscrimination law for employment and housing that protects LGBTQ+ people.

RELIGIOUS EXEMPTION

Foster and adoption agencies are sometimes religiously affiliated. Some of these organizations argue their religious beliefs allow them to reject foster or adoption applications from qualified LGBTQ+ adults. The United States was founded in part on the basis of religious freedom. Religious freedom means people cannot be discriminated against for their faith. In many instances,

The LGBTQ+ population often faces discrimination from religious organizations. These include religiously affiliated foster and adoption agencies and some health care providers.

religious freedom is an important federal protection. However, some activists argue there are times when religious freedom infringes on other people's rights.

Jennifer Pizer is the law and policy director at Lambda Legal. Lambda Legal is an organization that represents LGBTQ+ people in court. She says religious freedom is not the right term for the kind of discrimination that happens in foster and adoption agencies. In an article from 2018, Pizer said, "A more accurate term is 'religious exemption' or 'religious refusal.'" Pizer says that no politician wants to take away a person's right to practice their faith. However, she noted, "If they are operating a business that the state regulates to protect the public, then they must follow the law."[26] Religious exemptions often allow agencies to discriminate against more than just LGBTQ+ people. People who have been divorced, who are in interracial marriages, or who are single can be turned away. While federal protections for LGBTQ+ people do not exist, protections for other groups do.

Several laws allowing discrimination against LGBTQ+ people have been passed since the Supreme Court's decision to uphold LGBTQ+ marriage equality in 2015. States passed religious exemption bills to allow organizations to discriminate against LGBTQ+ couples and LGBTQ+ children. For example, in 2017, a South Dakota bill was passed. It provided protections for religious foster agencies. These protections allowed agencies to turn away LGBTQ+ foster parents. Agencies could also take away services from youth who were LGBTQ+.

These laws do little to protect children. Additionally, agencies rarely provide training for foster parents. Raising LGBTQ+ youth can be a challenge, especially when those youth may have been abused in their previous home. Trauma can cause children to act out. A foster family may not have the training to understand where the LGBTQ+ youth is coming from emotionally. This lack of understanding can create a hostile living environment. Religious exemption laws turn away qualified parents. As a result, there are fewer families to foster or adopt children. American Civil Liberties Union (ACLU) attorney Leslie Cooper said in an interview, "The people who bear the brunt of such [anti-LGBTQ+] laws are the children in the state foster care system who lose out on families that they desperately need."[27]

HEALTH CARE

Religious exemptions also affect health care. LGBTQ+ youth and adults have faced challenges in the health care industry

WORKING WITH RELIGION

Through social media and news representation, the prevailing view is that religious people, particularly Christians, reject queer sexualities and gender identities. The existence of organizations such as Exodus International aligns with this view. Exodus International is a Christian-based conversion therapy organization. Fundamentalist religions, or religions with unwavering attachment to certain beliefs, preach against homosexuality. The Westboro Baptist Church is known for picketing near pride parades. Pride parades celebrate LGBTQ+ identity. It is also true that youth who say they were kicked out of the house for their sexuality or gender identity are likely to come from religious households. These depictions are the norm in media. As a result, many people assume all religious people are anti-LGBTQ+.

A GLAAD study reported that three out of four mentions of LGBTQ+ people and religion in media and TV were negative in nature. The result is that LGBTQ+ and heterosexual people alike equate religion with anti-gay sentiments. Fair representations of pro-LGBTQ+ faith leaders is important for religious LGBTQ+ youth and for LGBTQ+ youth who come from religious households. Pro-LGBTQ+ religious organizations are becoming more prominent and vocal in their support of LGBTQ+ people.

for many years. Doctors have denied medication and care to people who are LGBTQ+. Doctors have turned away children of LGBTQ+ parents. LGBTQ+ youth, especially transgender youth, are misgendered by medical professionals. When a trans person is misgendered, that means someone uses the name and pronouns of their assigned sex, rather than their true gender. Reports exist of LGBTQ+ patients being released early from hospitals even when critical care was necessary.

Religious exemptions are not the only reasons LGBTQ+ people face discrimination in health care. Researchers say many doctors simply do not know how to care for LGBTQ+ patients. Kenneth Mayer is the research director at Fenway Institute. He says, "The biggest challenge is that the health care system is woefully unprepared to take appropriate care of LGBTQ people."[28]

> "The biggest challenge is that the health care system is woefully unprepared to take appropriate care of LGBTQ people."[28]
>
> —Kenneth Mayer, cochair and research director at Fenway Institute

Medical doctors are not the only health care providers who lack resources. Mental health professionals are also often undereducated. John Pachankis is the head of the Esteem Program at Yale, which studies how negative attitudes toward LGBTQ+ people can affect those people's mental health. While completing his PhD studies in

Many LGBTQ+ people avoid going to the doctor for fear of discrimination. While some discrimination is overt, some health care providers simply do not have training to adequately help LGBTQ+ people.

2008, he realized there was a lack of understanding among his colleagues regarding LGBTQ+ patients. In an interview, he said, "There has been this tragic lack in science, where we've taken much longer than we should have to create and deliver interventions that can reduce these mental health disparities." At the time, he was working with gay and bisexual men in New York. But he struggled to find resources both for himself and for his clients. In the interview, he continued, "There was no clear guidance on how to support these men in some of the

INTERSEX HEALTH CARE

Intersex people often face discrimination and a lack of information from health care professionals. Though several states are working to make the practice illegal, infant genital surgeries have been common in the past. Some intersex people are born with ambiguous genitalia. The practice of infant genital surgery serves to construct what doctors consider medically typical genitals on the infant. Subsequent surgeries are often required. However, for many intersex people, these surgeries were not wanted. Further, they are not medically necessary. There is nothing wrong with intersex people. The surgeries serve cosmetic purposes only. Later in life, intersex adolescents and adults must often play the role of educator for their doctors in order to receive necessary medical care. There is a lack of training for medical professionals surrounding informed care for intersex people.

unique difficulties they were going through."[29]

Discrimination and fear of discrimination prevents LGBTQ+ people from seeking medical care. LGBTQ+ people are more likely to postpone needed medical care for illness or injury, and they are more likely to postpone preventive screenings for possible diseases. As a result, LGBTQ+ people are more likely to suffer from preventable diseases because they did not or were not able to get the medical care they needed. Ryan Thoreson is a researcher at Human Rights Watch (HRW). In an interview in 2018, Thoreson said, "Discrimination puts LGBT people at heightened risk for a range of health issues, from depression and addiction to cancer and chronic conditions. Instead of treating those disparities as a public health issue, [the US Department of Health and Human Services] is developing politicized rules that will make them much worse."[30] Other patients report some services simply are not available for LGBTQ+ people. Respondents from another survey conducted in 2018 reported conversion efforts by doctors and nurses. One gay man wrote that after asking for an HIV test, his doctors "sat down and started preaching to me—not biblical things, but saying, you know this is not appropriate, I can help you with counseling, and I was like, oh, thank you, I've been out for 20 years and I think I'm okay. It's almost like they feel they have the right to tell you that it's wrong."[31]

According to a survey conducted by the Center for American Progress (CAP) in 2017, transgender patients were more likely to face discrimination than lesbian, gay, bisexual, and queer or questioning people. Transgender patients faced sexual assault in a doctor's office at four times the rate of those other groups. One transgender woman in Tennessee wrote in a survey from 2018, "I spent years looking for access to therapy and hormones and I just couldn't find it."[32]

The data collected by CAP also showed that finding a different health care provider was not necessarily a viable solution. Approximately 18 percent of respondents said it would be very difficult or impossible to find care at another hospital. In suburban or rural areas, LGBTQ+ people said they had even more trouble finding knowledgeable providers. There is often only one hospital in rural and suburban areas. As a result, 41 percent of survey respondents said it would be very difficult or impossible to find care at another hospital. Activists argue that the only way for LGBTQ+ people to receive equal, quality medical care is to create laws that protect them from discrimination.

LACKING PROTECTION

There have been significant strides in LGBTQ+ rights between 1970 and the present. Despite these improvements for the lives of LGBTQ+ people, a sweeping federal nondiscrimination law focused on LGBTQ+ rights did not exist by 2020. Many non-LGBTQ+ people are surprised to hear this. Naomi Goldberg is a policy research director for the Movement Advancement Project (MAP). She noted, "Most Americans are shocked to learn that we lack explicit laws protecting LGBTQ people from being fired for who they are or who they love."[33]

"Most Americans are shocked to learn that we lack explicit laws protecting LGBTQ people from being fired for who they are or who they love."[33]

—Naomi Goldberg, policy research director with Movement Advancement Project

Without federal protections, LGBTQ+ people can be denied housing. Employers can fire LGBTQ+ people for their sexual orientation or gender identity. Some politicians have argued

As of 2020, a federal nondiscrimination law protecting LGBTQ+ people did not exist. That means in some states, LGBTQ+ people can be fired from their jobs or denied housing or loans due to their identity.

that the clause that protects people from sex discrimination also includes gender and sexual identity. As a result, some US states do have protections for LGBTQ+ people. According to MAP, twenty-one states have nondiscrimination policies for employees that include sexual orientation and gender identity. In contrast, twenty-six states have no protections for employees. The numbers are similar for housing protections. However, when LGBTQ+ people apply for a credit card or loan, there are fewer protections. Only fourteen states protect all LGBTQ+ people from lending discrimination. This means that in most states, banks can deny LGBTQ+ people a loan or credit card because of their perceived or actual identity.

There are small and large effects when the United States does not have federal protections for LGBTQ+ people. Even those who live and work in areas that have nondiscrimination policies still face challenges. For example, one gay man said, "I'm trying to minimize the bias against me by changing my presentation in the corporate world. I lower my voice in meetings to make it sound less feminine and avoid wearing anything but a black suit. . . . When you're perceived as feminine— whether you're a woman or a gay man—you get excluded from relationships that improve your career."[34] Other people feel they cannot be their authentic selves at work. A queer woman in North Carolina said, "I wonder whether I would be let go if the higher-ups knew about my sexuality."[35] Fear of discrimination or violence keeps other LGBTQ+ people from applying to universities or jobs in states without protections. One student wrote, "I decided to apply to law schools only in LGBT-safe cities or states. I did not think I would be safe being an openly gay man. Especially a gay man of color, in some places."[36]

MEDIA REPRESENTATION

Many people turn to television and movies for an escape or to see themselves represented in the world; however, LGBTQ+

Media representation is important for LGBTQ+ youth. While LGBTQ+ representation has increased, representation is not always positive.

representation in the media is lacking. Few leading characters are LGBTQ+. And when LGBTQ+ characters are present, many end up dying onscreen. LGBTQ+ people are often not allowed happy endings in films.

Television and film producers use tropes for LGBTQ+ characters. A trope is an overused or cliché storyline. Tropes are similar to stereotypes. Both tropes and stereotypes affect LGBTQ+ characters. Generally, tropes and stereotypes serve to make fun of the LGBTQ+ character or advance another character's story. Rarely do tropes serve to help audiences better understand the LGBTQ+ character.

Some examples of tropes include the gay best friend, the transgender sex worker, and the coming-out storyline. While sharing an LGBTQ+ person's coming-out story or discussing sex work for transgender women is important, the focus of the narrative is often to help a straight character learn something new. The gay best friend trope is common in TV shows. One example is *Glee*'s Kurt. There are other common stereotypes seen in the media. Gay best friends are often effeminate gay men. They are sassy, and they are supposed to know how to dress. They may be dramatic or witty. Their main purpose is to provide comedic relief for the often-straight main character.

One of the most harmful tropes is nicknamed "bury your gays." This trope describes storylines in which a queer character, often female, is killed. *Orange Is the New Black*, *The 100*, *Pretty Little Liars*, and *The Walking Dead* all use this trope. The result of the bury your gays trope is that LGBTQ+ youth watch shows where the only future for people like them is death. GLAAD, formerly known as the Gay & Lesbian Alliance Against Defamation, is an organization that works for LGBTQ+ representation in media. GLAAD CEO Sarah Kate Ellis wrote,

Alycia Debnam-Carey played Lexa, an LGBTQ+ character on the CW's *The 100*. Lexa's death sparked outrage among fans, particularly for the circumstances in which it happened.

Most of these deaths served no other purpose than to further the narrative of a more central (and often straight, cisgender) character. When there are so few lesbian and bisexual women on television, the decision to kill these characters in droves sends a toxic message about the

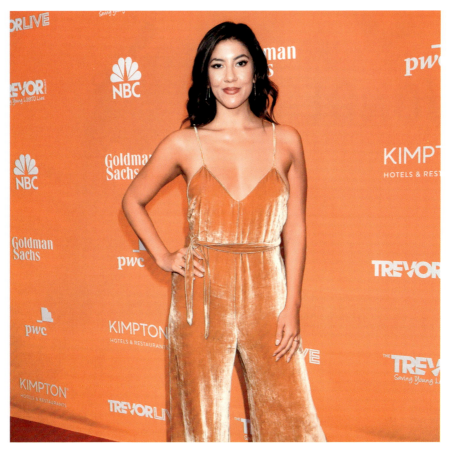

NBC's *Brooklyn Nine-Nine* is often praised for its positive LGBTQ+ representation. Stephanie Beatriz plays detective Rosa Diaz, who comes out as bisexual in the show's fifth season.

worth of queer female stories. When the most repeated ending for a queer woman is violent death, producers must do better to question the reason for a character's demise and what they are really communicating to the audience.[37]

The bury your gays trope is harmful, especially to youth. Emily Andras is the showrunner of the TV show *Wynonna Earp*.

She said, "All I see right now on social media is kids who are seeing themselves on television getting killed. If you live in a small town where you're already struggling to come out, or see yourself represented, that can do a lot of damage."

Fair media representation is important. It is one small step toward helping LGBTQ+ youth feel more supported. Andras went on to say, "I hope we get to the point where we have enough [gay] heroes, that we can also have amazing gay villains and amazing everything across the board. But right now, there is a bit of responsibility that we need to be aware of. I think we can write three-dimensional LGBT characters, and write better, more interesting, more unique stories. I really think we can."[38]

> "All I see right now on social media is kids who are seeing themselves on television getting killed. If you live in a small town where you're already struggling to come out, or see yourself represented, that can do a lot of damage."[38]
>
> —*Emily Andras, showrunner of* **Wynonna Earp**

More television series are exploring LGBTQ+ characters. David is a pansexual man on *Schitt's Creek*. Rosa Diaz comes out as bisexual on *Brooklyn Nine-Nine*. Taylor Mason from *Billions* and Theo Putnam on *The Chilling Adventures of Sabrina* are both nonbinary characters. Positive representation in the media plays an important role in making life better for LGBTQ+ youth.

CHAPTER FOUR

HOW DO WE ADDRESS THESE CHALLENGES?

LGBTQ+ youth continue to face challenges in school, at home, and in their communities. Easing those challenges is not a simple process. However, through policy changes and education, LGBTQ+ youth will face less social stigma. When LGBTQ+ youth feel supported by their families and communities, they are healthier both physically and mentally.

AT HOME

One of the most stressful times in an LGBTQ+ youth's life is when they are coming out. Fear of rejection can keep youth from telling their parents about their gender identity or sexual orientation. In order for LGBTQ+ youth to be as happy and healthy as possible, it is important for them to be able to live authentically. That means being able to be out at home and in their community.

Community and family support for LGBTQ+ youth is key to reducing social stigma. This leads to better physical and mental health for LGBTQ+ youth.

Creating a supportive environment for LGBTQ+ youth is an important step that parents can take. Psychiatrist Jonathan Tobkes said that parents need to know how to respond in a supportive way. He noted, "There are still things you can and should do to provide your child with the comfort and stability that are crucial in leading to a positive outcome. In other words, you can say the right things even if you are not fully at peace with the situation. Ask your child the same questions you would ask your other children. Specifically, don't avoid the topic of dating and relationships."[39] Avoiding these topics creates a feeling that an LGBTQ+ youth's identity is wrong. Parents need to take an interest in their queer child's life in the same way they would if their child was heterosexual and cisgender.

Not all parents understand their child's sexual orientation or gender identity. There may be new terms to learn. Parents may even feel sad. Many parents have expectations for their child. When their child comes out as queer or trans, they must learn to let go of those expectations. But it is an important step that all parents must take. One parent of an LGBTQ+ child said in an interview,

> When your child comes out to you, it's going to be a big change for you. The road that you see for your child will become more difficult, and that can be a painful thing to be aware of. You will be introduced to a whole new world and a new life that is going to take some getting used to, and you may have to learn some unfamiliar terminology for your child. Be patient with yourself. . . . But above all, accept your child, and always love them. Never stop loving them, and never forget to tell them how much you love them.[40]

Parents may have questions or concerns when their child comes out as LGBTQ+. Resources such as PFLAG help answer questions and teach parents how to be supportive.

When LGBTQ+ youth have a supportive home environment, their mental health is much better. They are at a significantly lower risk of depression and suicide. When LGBTQ+ youth have family they can count on, they are better equipped to handle other forms of stigma in the community. Parents can join or get information from their local PFLAG chapter. PFLAG is a resource for parents and allies of LGBTQ+ youth.

IN SCHOOL

The average student spends thirty-three hours per week in school. This number accounts only for the school day. It does

TITLE IX

Title IX is a nondiscrimination amendment. It protects students from discrimination based on sex. It was signed in 1972. Title IX guaranteed that male and female students could participate in the same school activities.

In 2011, courts ruled that Title IX also protected LGBTQ+ teens. The ruling stated that protections extended beyond a person's sex. The protections included the societal expectations of what a person should look like and how they should act. For example, a bisexual male student would be expected to dress in traditional, masculine clothing and date girls. If that student goes against those expectations, he is still protected under the regulations of Title IX. As of 2019, no student in public schools may be discriminated against for their sexuality or gender identity and expression. But for many LGBTQ+ students, the definition of discrimination can be muddy. Court cases regarding the reach and limit of Title IX protections continue.

not take into consideration extracurriculars such as sports or theater. LGBTQ+ youth need to feel safe in school. Without protections, LGBTQ+ youth face an increased risk of being bullied and harassed. This leads to LGBTQ+ students skipping school and worsens their mental health outcomes. But educators and policymakers can help.

Individual schools, school districts, and states all have policies to protect students from bullying and unfair treatment. Some states and schools have comprehensive policies, with antibullying and antidiscrimination rules that protect all students, including LGBTQ+ students. Other schools and states do not. But even if states do not have comprehensive policies, schools can make their own. Protecting LGBTQ+ students creates a safer school environment for all students.

One thing schools can do is support LGBTQ+ student organizations. GSAs help LGBTQ+ students and their allies find a community in school. These groups foster activism. Students work to educate peers and staff about LGBTQ+ issues. Between 2001 and 2015, GLSEN's National School Climate Survey found LGBTQ+ students' access to GSAs had increased. In 2001, only 20 percent of LGBTQ+ students said their school had a GSA. In 2015, 60 percent of respondents said their school had one.

GSAs help create a safer school environment. Emily Greytak, director of research for GLSEN, said, "One of the key benefits of a GSA is that it can provide a link between straight and non-straight peers. We have found that having a GSA in school is directly related to students being more accepting of LGBT people, less anti-LGBT language [being heard] and increased student safety—particularly for LGBTQ students."[41] Geoffrey Winder, co-executive director of GSA Network, echoed this in an interview. He said, "Trans and queer student organizers have shared compelling personal accounts about how their GSA clubs create safe spaces in schools and serve as powerful vehicles for social change on campus."[42]

Safe schools allow students to focus on their

> "Trans and queer student organizers have shared compelling personal accounts about how their GSA clubs create safe spaces in schools and serve as powerful vehicles for social change on campus."[42]
>
> —*Geoffrey Winder, co-executive director of GSA Network*

GSAs help foster safer school environments for LGBTQ+ youth. GLSEN found that student access to GSAs increased significantly from 2001 to 2015.

classes instead of whether they can use the restroom or will get bullied in the lunchroom. GSAs also provide LGBTQ+ students with a community of other LGBTQ+-identified peers. In an interview, one student said, "High school can be really tough, knowing that I had people who were going through the same struggles that I was, gay or not, really helped me get through it."[43]

Administrators can support LGBTQ+ students by helping them create student-led organizations. Sometimes, school staff must act in the best interest of the student. For example, staff should not tell guardians about a student's name or pronoun change. GLSEN has developed a Model District Policy on Transgender and Gender Nonconforming Students. It says, "It is critical that parental/guardian approval is never a prerequisite for respecting a student's chosen name, appropriate gender, and pronouns. . . . Staff should take guidance from and work collaboratively with the student to ensure that the student remains safe, both at school and at home."[44] Not all students feel they can come out to their parents. Some may simply not be ready to. Outing a student to their parents by telling the parents of the student's sexual orientation or gender identity could put the student in danger. Staff do not know what the student's home environment is like. If parents are not supportive of their LGBTQ+ child, the student could face abuse or other forms of rejection. Respecting a transgender student's name and pronouns sets the example for the whole student body.

Teachers, too, play a large role in helping LGBTQ+ students feels safe at school. All teachers have the ability to become better allies. GLSEN's *Safe Space Kit* has information to help teachers support their LGBTQ+ students. It says, "One of the most important parts of being an ally to LGBTQ students is making yourself known as an ally. In order to come to you for help, students need to be able to recognize you as an ally."[45] But being an ally takes work. It is not always enough for teachers to say they are an ally. Becca Mui, GLSEN's Education Manager, discussed this in an interview. She said:

One of the things that is tricky about LGBTQ and trans identities when people are not part of those communities is that that language is changing, specifically the language we're using to talk about gender. It is literally my job to be connected, to be supportive, to know what's going on, and I'm constantly finding out that something's been updated, something's been changed. Having the attitude that we use the language we have and we are open to learning that something's been updated can be really useful.[46]

All people are continuing to learn. Teachers can set an example. They can take it upon themselves to continue to ask questions and educate themselves.

Asking students is one way teachers can continue to learn. But teachers should not rely only on students. That puts a lot of pressure on LGBTQ+ youth who may still be figuring things

Teachers can be important allies for LGBTQ+ students. Teachers can show they are allies by learning about LGBTQ+ issues and supporting their LGBTQ+ students.

out themselves. Teachers can look for information online. GLSEN is a resource specifically for educators and students.

IN THE COMMUNITY

Supportive families and schools are two important parts of lessening challenges for LGBTQ+ youth. Another aspect is the community. Safe schools and loving families can protect LGBTQ+ youth from many risk factors. But there are still areas in

Community support is important for LGBTQ+ youth. This includes support from the health care community and banning conversion therapy.

society where LGBTQ+ youth do not receive adequate services. These include health care and youth homelessness.

Strides are occurring both in mental health support and in medical care. Providing safe and informed health care for LGBTQ+ teens allows them to create healthier habits as adults. Medical doctors are beginning to receive more training in how to care for LGBTQ+ youth and adults. Health care forms now often include an area for a person's name and pronouns if they are different from the ones assigned at birth.

Mental health support is also improving. One of the most important developments is the banning of conversion therapy in some areas. As of March 2020, twenty states have banned conversion therapy. Many more cities have created legislation to stop conversion therapy within city limits. Banning conversion therapy and educating mental health providers allows LGBTQ+ youth to feel confident in their identities. Marcus Waterbury, a transgender activist, gave a speech at Minnesota's Mall of America in December 2019. The event raised money for LGBTQ+ youth. In the speech, Waterbury said,

> What we have found is that when you have transgender and gender nonconforming youth who are supported by the people around them, they are less likely to be discriminated against in the wider world. They are more confident, less fearful, and they carry themselves different[ly]. So that is why funding mental health services for these youth, ages thirteen to twenty-three, is really key.[47]

In addition to informed health care, activists are working toward improving care for homeless LGBTQ+ youth and LGBTQ+ youth in foster care. Several organizations have created information packets for foster parents of LGBTQ+ youth.

The United States celebrates Pride Month in the month of June. Cities hold parades and other celebrations of LGBTQ+ rights.

LGBTQ+ youth in foster care are looking for support and patience. One foster child said, "At [my foster mother's] house, I was able to feel safe and focus on being who I was."[48]

Bryan Samuels is the former Commissioner for the US Administration on Children, Youth and Families. In a statement regarding LGBTQ+ youth in foster care, he said, "Every child and youth who is unable to live with his or her parents is entitled to a safe, loving and affirming foster care placement, irrespective of the young person's sexual orientation, gender identity or gender expression."[49]

Additionally, June is national LGBTQ+ Pride Month in the United States. Many pride parades happen in the month of June across the United States. Pride celebrations are a chance to increase LGBTQ+ visibility for people who have been out for many years, as well as for those who have not been able to safely come out. Celebrating LGBTQ+ identities provides hope and joy for LGBTQ+ youth around the United States.

There are many challenges for LGBTQ+ teens. However, social acceptance and policy changes are helping to create more supportive environments. In time, many LGBTQ+ activists hope that this progress will make their activism unnecessary. LGBTQ+ adults remind teens that it takes time, but challenges lessen. Schuyler Bailar is a transgender member of Harvard University's swim team. In an Instagram caption, he wrote: "Change is possible. Happiness is possible. Authenticity is possible. But all of these things take time and effort and perseverance and self-love. Still, they are ever possible; so, never forget this, my friends. Never give up on yourselves."[50]

"Change is possible. Happiness is possible. Authenticity is possible. But all of these things take time and effort and perseverance and self-love. Still, they are ever possible; so, never forget this, my friends. Never give up on yourselves."[50]

—Schuyler Bailar, a transgender swimmer at Harvard

SOURCE NOTES

INTRODUCTION: CHALLENGES FOR LGBTQ+ TEENS

1. Quoted in "500 Queer Scientists to Make Your Day Smarter," *Advocate*, n.d. www.advocate.com.

2. Quoted in Mandy Stadtmiller, "You Might Be Sexually Fluid and Not Realize It—Or Even Care," *Mashable*, May 18, 2015. www.mashable.com.

3. Quoted in Sarah Marsh, "The Gender-Fluid Generation: Young People on Being Male, Female or Non-Binary," *Guardian*, March 23, 2016. www.theguardian.com.

4. Quoted in Katie Dupere, "10 Trans and Gender-Nonconforming Youth Activists of Color Changing the World," *Mashable*, June 30, 2017. www.mashable.com.

CHAPTER 1: WHAT ARE THE CHALLENGES?

5. Quoted in "The Challenges and Opportunities for LGBT Rights," *Northwestern*, March 4, 2019. https://ipr.northwestern.edu.

6. Quoted in "The 2017 National School Climate Survey," *GLSEN*, 2017. www.glsen.org.

7. Quoted in "Like Walking Through a Hailstorm," *Human Rights Watch*, December 7, 2016. www.hrw.org.

8. Quoted in Will Hall, "Harassment, Bullying, & Discrimination of Lesbian, Gay, Bisexual, & Transgender Students," *SafeSchoolsNC*, 2007. www.publiccharters.org.

9. Quoted in "The 2017 National School Climate Survey."

10. Quoted in "The 2017 National School Climate Survey."

11. Quoted in "United States: LGBT Students Face Discrimination," *Human Rights Watch*, December 7, 2016. www.hrw.org.

12. Quoted in Hall, "Harassment, Bullying, & Discrimination."

13. Quoted in "Like Walking Through a Hailstorm."

14. Quoted in "The 2017 National School Climate Survey."

15. Jessica Valenti, "Homophobic, Transphobic Parents Make Abusive Homes. Let's Help LGBT Kids Get Out," *Guardian*, January 5, 2015. www.theguardian.com.

CHAPTER 2: HOW DO THESE CHALLENGES AFFECT TEENS?

16. Quoted in Elizabeth Sutherland, "What Is Minority Stress and How Do We Deal with It?" *SBS*, April 7, 2016. https://sbs.com.au.

17. Quoted in "Like Walking Through a Hailstorm."

18. Quoted in Brynn Tannehill, "The Truth About Transgender Suicide," *HuffPost*, November 14, 2015. www.huffpost.com.

19. Quoted in "Conversion Therapy Survivors' Statement," *Conversion Therapy Survivors*, n.d. www.conversiontherapysurvivors.org.

20. Quoted in Janice Wood, "Conversion Therapy for LGBT Kids Linked to Higher Risks of Depression & Suicide," *PsychCentral*, November 12, 2018. www.psychcentral.com.

21. Quoted in Wood, "Conversion Therapy for LGBT Kids."

22. Quoted in Sam Sanchez, "Transgender Teens Struggle in Foster Care," *San Antonio Current*, March 16, 2015. www.sacurrent.com.

23. Quoted in Stell Simonton, "LGBTQ, Traumatized Homeless Youth More Vulnerable to Being Trafficked: Report," *YouthToday*, October 21, 2019. www.youthtoday.org.

24. Quoted in Maya Rhodan, "Report Sheds New Light on Lives of Homeless Gay Youth," *Time*, February 25, 2015. www.time.com.

25. Quoted in Charlotte Clymer, "HRC President to Congress: Anti-LGBTQ Housing Discrimination Is 'Morally Bankrupt,'" *Human Rights Campaign*, October 29, 2019. www.hrc.org.

CHAPTER 3: HOW DO THESE CHALLENGES AFFECT SOCIETY?

26. Quoted in Mike Albo, "Religious Freedom," *Lambda Legal*, n.d. www.lambdalegal.org.

SOURCE NOTES CONTINUED

27. Quoted in Samantha Allen, "These States Want to Make LGBT Adoption as Hard as Possible," *Daily Beast*, April 24, 2018. www.thedailybeast.com.

28. Quoted in Alvin Powell, "The Problems with LGBTQ Health Care," *Harvard Gazette*, March 23, 2018. https://news.harvard.edu.

29. Quoted in Tori DeAngelis, "Treating the Effects of LGBT Stigma," *American Psychological Association*, February 2018. www.apa.org.

30. Quoted in "US: LGBT People Face Healthcare Barriers," *Human Rights Watch*, July 23, 2018. www.hrw.org.

31. Quoted in "US: LGBT People Face Healthcare Barriers."

32. Quoted in "US: LGBT People Face Healthcare Barriers."

33. Quoted in Susan Miller, "'Shocking' Numbers: Half of LGBTQ Adults Live in States Where No Laws Ban Job Discrimination," *USA Today*, October 8, 2019. www.usatoday.com.

34. Quoted in Sejal Singh and Laura E. Durso, "Widespread Discrimination Continues to Shape LGBT People's Lives in Both Subtle and Significant Ways," *Center for American Progress*, May 2, 2017. www.americanprogress.org.

35. Quoted in Singh and Durso, "Widespread Discrimination."

36. Quoted in Singh and Durso, "Widespread Discrimination."

37. Quoted in Alamin Yohannes, "'Bury Your Gays': Why Are So Many Lesbian TV Characters Dying Off?" *NBC News*, November 4, 2016. www.nbcnews.com.

38. Quoted in Emma Dibdin, "TV Writers Need to Stop Killing Off Their Gay Characters," *Marie Claire*, August 9, 2017. www.marieclaire.com.

CHAPTER 4: HOW DO WE ADDRESS THESE CHALLENGES?

39. Quoted in Jonathan L. Tobkes, M.D., and Wesley C. Davidson, "Why Does the LGBT Community Experience More Drug Abuse?" *Psychology Today*, July 6, 2017. www.psychologytoday.com.

40. Quoted in "To the Parents of LGBTQ+ Kids," *GLSEN*, n.d. www.glsen.org.

41. Quoted in Lyndsey D'Arcangelo, "Gay-Straight Alliances More Important Than Ever, Advocates Say," *NBC News*, February 10, 2017. www.nbcnews.com.

42. Quoted in "GSA Clubs Protect LGBTQ+ Students from Bias-Based Bullying, Study Shows," *GSA Network*, May 13, 2019. www.gsanetwork.org.

43. Quoted in D'Arcangelo, "Gay-Straight Alliances More Important Than Ever."

44. Quoted in "Model District Policy on Transgender and Gender Nonconforming Students," *GLSEN*, n.d. www.glsen.org.

45. Quoted in "Safe Space Kit," *GLSEN*, 2016. www.glsen.org.

46. Quoted in Jennifer Gonzalez, "Making School a Safe Place for LGBTQ Students," *Cult of Pedagogy*, November 5, 2017. www.cultofpedagogy.com.

47. Quoted in Joelle Goldstein, "Minnesota Mall of America Store Raises $1K for LGBTQ Youth amid Conversion Therapy Ban," *Yahoo! Entertainment*, December 17, 2019. www.yahoo.com.

48. Quoted in "Supporting Your LGBTQ Youth: A Guide for Foster Parents," *Child Welfare Information Gateway*, May 2013. www.childwelfare.gov.

49. Quoted in "Caring for LGBTQ Children & Youth," *Human Rights Campaign*, n.d. www.hrc.org.

50. Quoted in Rosemary Donahue, "Transgender Teen Shares Powerful Prom Photos Taken Three Years Apart," *Allure*, May 18, 2017. www.allure.com.

FOR FURTHER RESEARCH

BOOKS

A.W. Buckey, *LGBT Intolerance*. San Diego, CA: ReferencePoint Press, 2020.

Leanne Currie-McGhee, *LGBT Families*. San Diego, CA: ReferencePoint Press, 2019.

Duchess Harris and Kristin Marciniak, *LGBTQ Discrimination in America*. Minneapolis, MN: Abdo Publishing, 2020.

Duchess Harris and Rebecca Rowell, *Growing Up LGBTQ*. Minneapolis, MN: Abdo Publishing, 2020.

Don Nardo, *Thinking Critically: LGBT Issues*. San Diego, CA: ReferencePoint Press, 2020.

INTERNET SOURCES

Tara Bahrampour, "Becoming Eli," *Washington Post*, December 20, 2019. www.washingtonpost.com.

Alexander Leon, "LGBT People Are Prone to Mental Illness. It's a Truth We Shouldn't Shy Away From," *Guardian*, May 12, 2017. www.theguardian.com.

"LGBT Youth," *Centers for Disease Control and Prevention*, June 21, 2017. www.cdc.gov.

WEBSITES

GLAAD
www.glaad.org

GLAAD is an organization that works toward equality and fair representation of LGBTQ+ people in the media.

GLSEN
www.glsen.org

GLSEN is a resource for educators and students. It provides information about how teachers can create a safe space for LGBTQ+ students at their school, and it provides resources for gay-straight alliances.

The Trevor Project
www.thetrevorproject.org

The Trevor Project is a suicide prevention site for LGBTQ+ youth. It has information about suicide and other LGBTQ+ issues as well as a hotline and text-line for youth in crisis. If you or someone you know is struggling with suicidality, please reach out. The Trevor Lifeline has counselors available twenty-four hours a day: 1-866-488-7386.

INDEX

INDEX CONTINUED

IMAGE CREDITS

ABOUT THE AUTHOR

Martha Lundin is a genderqueer author and educator. Martha uses the gender-neutral pronouns they/them. They write books for young readers full-time.